level 2

FA~

CLASSIC MELODIES

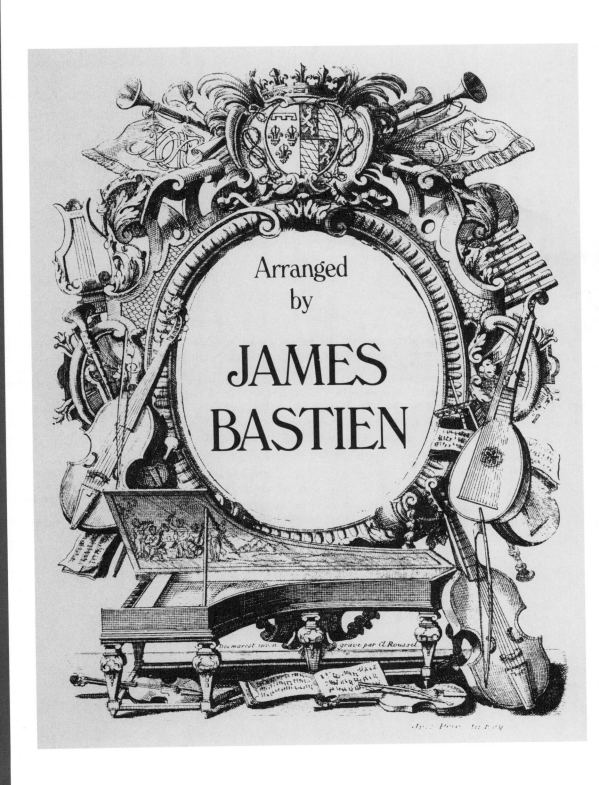

Arranged
by

JAMES
BASTIEN

KJOS WEST • Neil A. Kjos Music Company, Publisher • San Diego, California

PREFACE

Favorite Classic Melodies (Primer Level through Level 4) provides a source of learning and enjoyment representing the major works for the symphony, opera, chorus, and piano. These books may be used in conjunction with any piano course for supplementary enrichment.

Suggested Use of Materials with "PIANO LESSONS, Level 2."

After completing **page 5,** the student is ready to begin .... Theory Lessons-Level 2 (WP8)
After completing **page 7,** the student is ready to begin .... Technic Lessons-Level 2 (WP13)
After completing **page 13,** the student is ready to begin .... Piano Solos-Level 2 (WP24)
After completing **page 15,** the student is ready to begin .... Sight Reading-Level 2 (WP17)
After completing **page 18,** the student is ready to begin
these Supplementary Books .... Bastien Favorites-Level 2 (GP84)
Duet Favorites-Level 2 (WP61)
Christmas Favorites-Level 2 (WP50)
Christmas Duets-Level 2 (GP312)
Favorite Classic Melodies-Level 2 (WP74)
Hymn Favorites-Level 2 (WP45)
Piano Recital Solos-Level 2 (WP66)
Pop Piano Styles-Level 2 (WP52)

SHEET MUSIC from **Level Two Solos** may be assigned to the student at the teacher's discretion.

ISBN 0-8497-5129-2

Published by Kjos West.
Distributed by Neil A. Kjos Music Company.
National Order Desk, 4382 Jutland Dr., San Diego, CA 92117

CONTENTS

March Militaire

Franz Schubert
arr. by James Bastien

Tempo di marcia

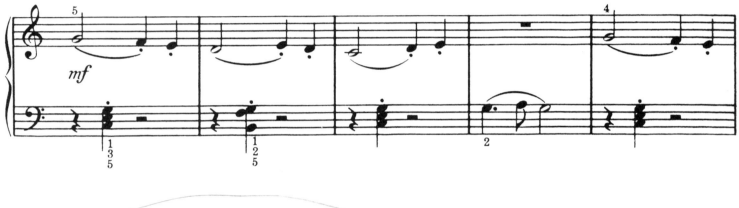

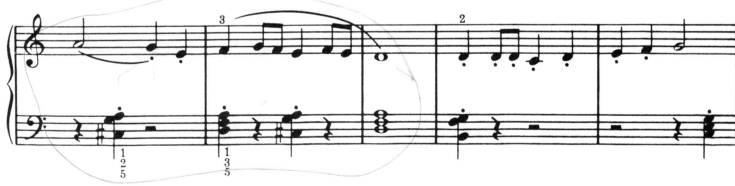

© 1981 Kjos West, San Diego, Calif.
International Copyright Secured   All Rights Reserved   Printed in U.S.A.

WP74

This Arrangement © 1980 Kjos West, San Diego, California

Roses from the South

Johann Strauss, Jr.
arr. by James Bastien

Wedding March

from "A Midsummer Night's Dream"

Felix Mendelssohn
arr. by James Bastien

Moderato

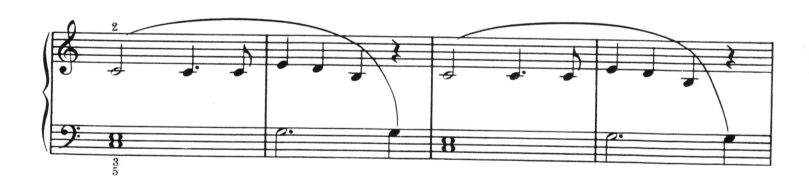

Lullaby

Johannes Brahms
arr. by James Bastien

The Blue Danube Waltz

Johann Strauss, Jr.
arr. by James Bastien

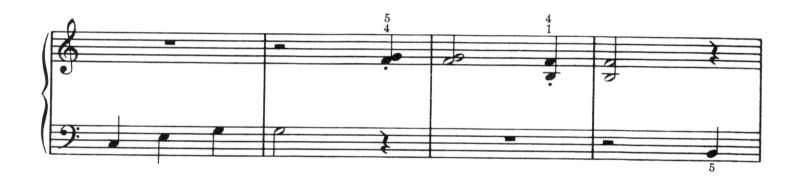

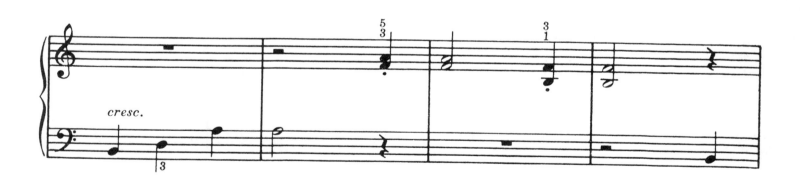

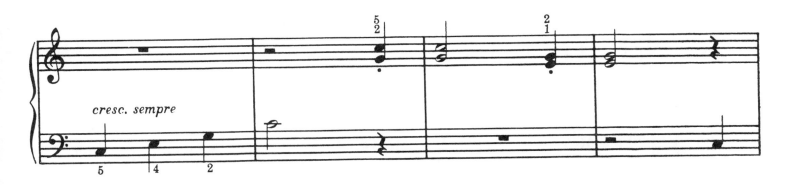

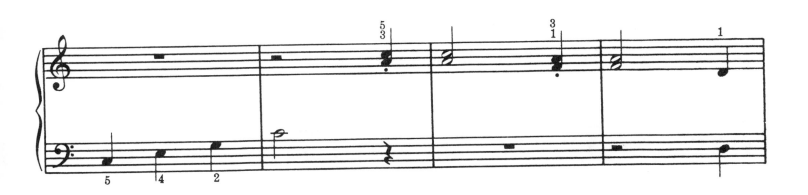

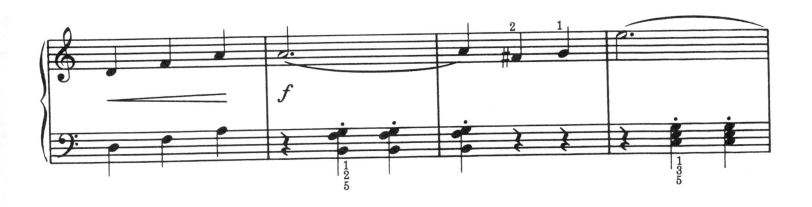

To a Wild Rose

Edward MacDowell
arr. by James Bastien

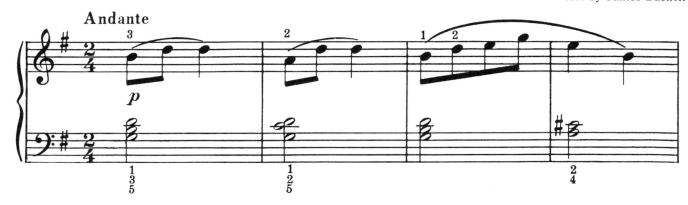

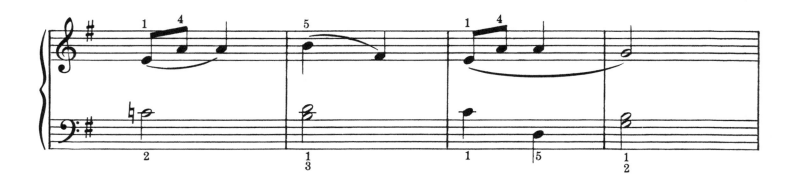

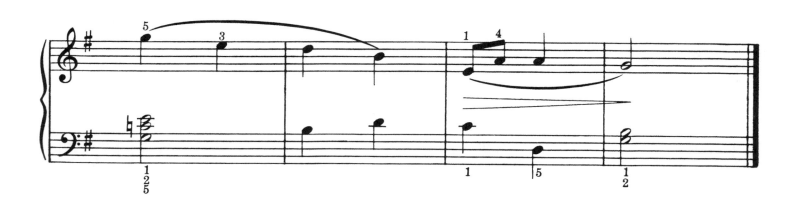

Bourrée

Johann Sebastian Bach
arr. by James Bastien

Allegro moderato

The Merry Farmer

Robert Schumann
arr. by James Bastien

Für Elise

Ludwig van Beethoven
arr. by James Bastien

With motion

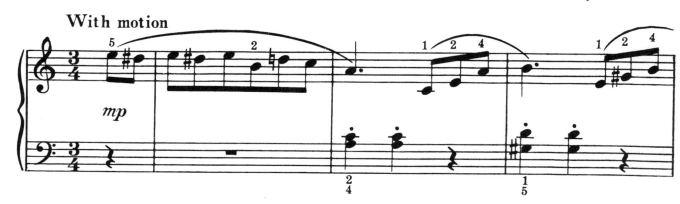

Barcarolle

from the opera "Tales of Hoffman"

Jacques Offenbach
arr. by James Bastien

In the Hall of the Mountain King

from "Peer Gynt Suite"

Edvard Grieg
arr. by James Bastien

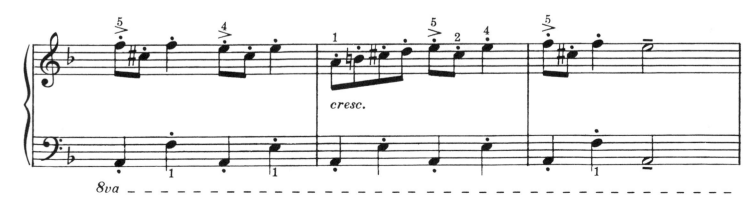

WP74

Wooden Shoe Dance

from the opera "Hansel and Gretel"

Engelbert Humperdinck
arr. by James Bastien

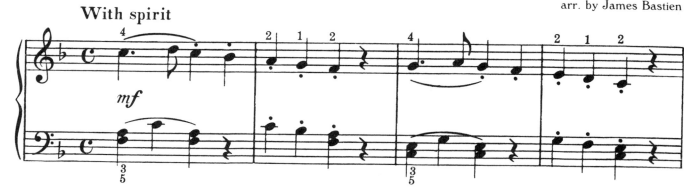

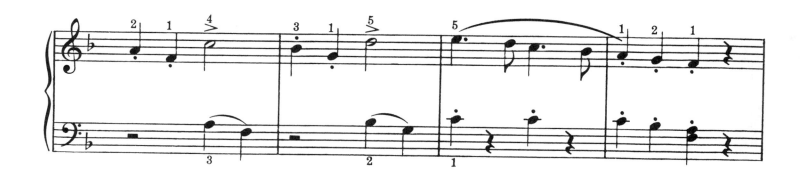

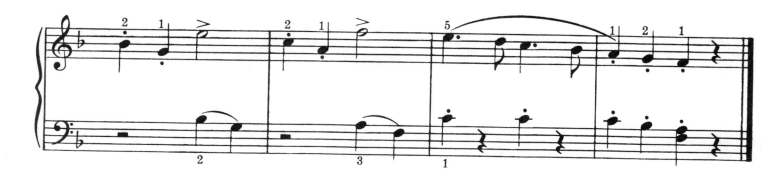

Hallelujah Chorus

from the "Messiah"

George Frideric Handel
arr. by James Bastien

Allegro maestoso

Saint Anthony Chorale

Theme

Joseph Haydn
arr. by James Bastien